Roman City GUIDE BOOK

Jill Laidlaw

Published 2009 by
A & C Black Publishers Ltd.
36 Soho Square, London, W1D 3QY
www.acblack.com

ISBN HB 978-1-4081-0862-8
       PB   978-1-4081-1289-2

Series consultant: Gill Matthews

A CIP catalogue for this book is available from the British Library.

This book is produced using paper that is made from wood grown in managed, sustainable forests. It is natural, renewable and recyclable. The logging and manufacturing processes conform to the environmental regulations of the country of origin.

Produced for A & C Black by Calcium.
Printed and bound in China by C&C Offset Printing Co.

All the internet addresses given in this book were correct at the time of going to press. The author and publishers regret any inconvenience caused if addresses have changed or sites have ceased to exist, but can accept no responsibility for any such changes.

Acknowledgements
The publishers would like to thank the following for their kind permission to reproduce their photographs:
Cover: Fotolia: Tinka; Istockphoto: Thomas Pullicino; Shutterstock: Cornel Achirei, Ljupco Smokovski, Pippa West. **Pages:** Alamy: The London Art Archive 20; Bridgeman Art Library: Heini Schneebeli 18, Verulamium Museum 21; Corbis: Vanni Archive 4; Istockphoto: Thomas Pullicino 15b; Photoshot: De Agostini/World Illustrated 13; Rex Features: Collection 12, Sipa Press 11; Shutterstock: Danilo Ascione 7t, Matthew Collingwood 19, Dragunov 17t, Laurence Gough 8l, Gul 5, Javarman 10b, Marivlada 10t, Massimo Merlini 16, Andre Nantel 14, Clara Natoli 15t, 17b, Kenneth V. Pilon 9t, Ruta Saulyte-Laurinaviciene 9b, Tomasz Szymanski 8r, Khirman Vladimir 7b.
Illustration: Geoff Ward 6.

CONTENTS

THE CITY CENTRE

Welcome to Rome in AD 200. It is the largest, most famous city in the world – a million people live here.

This is Rome from above. It is one of the most incredible cities in the world.

Finding your way

Rome has grown bigger and bigger over hundreds of years. Now it's a mess of thousands of streets, in which you can easily get lost. In the newer areas, however, streets have been built in a grid pattern that is easier to follow.

Colosseum

Circus Maximus

Slave city

You will see a lot of slaves in Rome. The city depends on them. Slaves cook, clean, garden, and look after children. They even empty the toilet jars that men and boys use in the streets!

The Forum of the Romans

The Forum is one of Rome's main meeting places. The crowded streets open out into a big space jammed with crowds of people shouting their business.

You can watch acrobats, listen to musicians play, and even have your fortune told.

We Romans have a vast empire, stretching all over the world. People from all over the empire come to visit Rome.

5

WHERE TO STAY

The cheapest places to stay are blocks of flats, called *insulae*. They can be dangerous. Criminals find *insulae* easy to rob. *Insulae* are very crowded and sometimes fall down without warning. Get a room on the ground floor or first floor, so you can get out if there is a fire.

Up-market

It is much nicer to stay in a house – there is less noise for a start. Richer people, such as **merchants**, live in houses with a courtyard in the middle with a garden. We Romans call a house a *domus*.

Insulae are made of stone and wood. They often catch fire and burn down.

Room for rent

People advertise rooms in their houses for travellers to rent. Look for a sign on the wall of the house.

The inside of a *domus* can be beautifully decorated with wall paintings and mosaics.

Five-star stays

Our richest citizens live like gods. They have town houses and also **villas** (such as the one below). They are usually outside the city, away from all the noises and smells.

SHOPPING

Rome is a very good place for shopping. We Romans built the Markets of **Trajan**, the world's first shopping centre. It has 150 offices and shops that sell things like flowers, jewellery, wool, wine, and food.

Rainbow-coloured mosaics

Some of these shops are beautiful. Pictures of the goods on sale are set into the walls or floors. They are made of tiny pieces of brightly coloured tiles. These pictures are called mosaics.

Fish is very expensive in Rome. Wine is cheap.

Earning a living

Roman money is called *denarii*.
A Roman soldier earns about
450 *denarii* a year. It costs about
15 *denarii* to buy a pair of boots.

Shopping tips

- Look for shops in the bottom of buildings, along the street.
- For the freshest food go to one of the markets held every nine days for all the farmers who live outside Rome.

Souvenirs

Some things you can buy on the streets:

- live animals in cages
- slaves
- silk from China
- wool from France
- spices from India

Romans use spices
from India to
flavour their food.

EATING OUT

We have thousands of fast food stalls, called *thermopolia*. These stalls are open to the street. Their counters are filled with take-away hot food and drink.

Olive oil is used to cook most foods in Rome.

Delicacies

Some of our favourite foods are:

- dolphin meatballs
- boiled parrot
- jellyfish omelettes
- stuffed dormice
- crows

Bread snacks

You will see large bread ovens all over the city. We love bread and call it *panis* (right). We dip it in wine or olive oil and eat it as a snack because we do not eat a big meal until the late afternoon.

Banquets

If you are lucky you might be invited to a **banquet**. Banquets take place in people's houses. It is usual to eat a banquet lying down on couches arranged around a table. Banquets can last for hours.

Food and wine is served at banquets by slaves.

Banquet manners

- Eat with your fingers.
- Take your own napkin.

CHARIOT RACES

Chariot racing is the most popular sport in Rome. Screaming crowds cheer on their heroes.

Chariot driving is a dangerous sport. Many horses and drivers die in crashes.

The Circus Maximus

The Circus Maximus is a huge stadium where people flock to see chariot racing. About 200,000 people can fit into the Circus Maximus.

A chariot driver races with the reins wrapped around his waist.

How do they do it?

Drivers stand on small wooden platforms fixed above the wheels of the chariots. They wrap the **reins** around their waists, then lean in different directions to control their horses.

Which team do you support?

- There are usually four chariot teams in a race.
- Each team has three chariots.
- The team colours are green, blue, white, or red.
- Fans wear team colours.
- The charioteers usually race around the Circus Maximus seven times.

Top earners

Top chariot drivers can earn as much as a schoolteacher does in a year – for winning just one race!

GLADIATORS

About once a month you can see gladiators fight in the Colosseum. This is a massive oval arena, called an **amphitheatre**.

Up to 80,000 people can fit in the Colosseum.

How to take part

If you want to help decide if a gladiator lives or dies you'll need to learn a few words of **Latin**.

- *Mitte* means "Let him go."
- *Iu-gula!* means "Kill!"

Gladiators are trained to fight at special schools.

Gladiator guide

Gladiators are stars. They are also slaves and criminals. Here are four of the most popular types of gladiator.

- *Mirmillones*: have a helmet with a fish crest, an oblong shield, and a sword. They can be put with a *Thracian* or a *Retiarii* to fight as a team.
- *Retiarii*: have very few weapons, only a net and either a **trident** or a dagger.
- *Samnites*: have a short sword, a helmet, and an oblong shield.
- *Thracians*: have a curved sword and a round shield.

15

GUIDE TO GODS

The gods here in Rome all have superpowers. We pray to them and give **sacrifices** to make sure they stay here and protect us.

The walls of the Pantheon are 7 m (20 ft) thick so they can carry the huge weight of the dome.

The Pantheon

The **Pantheon** is the temple where all the main gods live. It is huge. The roof is a dome, like an open umbrella stuck on top of the building.

MAGRIPPALFCOSTERTIVI

Pleasing the gods

Priests kill animals such as bulls or chickens. Then they cut them open. If the insides are healthy, the gods are happy. If the insides are unhealthy, the gods are angry.

Neptune is the Roman god of seas, horses, and earthquakes.

Top gods

Jupiter: king of the gods

Juno: queen of the gods

Venus: goddess of love

Diana: goddess of hunting/ the moon

Apollo: god of the sun

Mars: god of war

Minerva: goddess of warriors

Neptune: god of the sea

Mercury: messenger of the gods

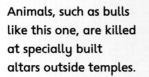

Animals, such as bulls like this one, are killed at specially built altars outside temples.

A LEISURELY BATH

Rome is a smelly, hot, noisy city but there is an easy way to keep clean – have a bath! We have public baths that are the wonder of the world – up to 1,000 people can bathe at one time.

How to have a Roman bath

1. Take your clothes off and do a few exercises.
2. Then go into another room, called the "warm room" or *tepidarium*, which is filled with hot air.
3. Next, go into the *calidarium*, the "hot room". It is so hot it is like being in a fire! Rub perfumed oil onto your skin and then scrape it off.
4. Finally, jump into the *frigidarium*, a pool of freezing water.

A *strigil* is a scraper that clears away oil, sweat, dirt, and dead skin. It has a handle and a curved blade.

Some things to do at the baths

- Bathe!
- Do business
- Eat
- Read (baths have libraries)
- Have a beauty treatment
- Just relax!

There are almost 900 public baths in Rome!

IF YOU ARE ILL...

So many people live in Rome that illness can quickly spread through the city from person to person.

Stay well

If you feel ill or are injured in a fall from a chariot, there is no hospital to go to. There is a hospital at the military camp, but only soldiers are allowed to use it.

Finding a doctor

Try to find a doctor who is a captured Greek slave – they are much better than Roman doctors. Some doctors even try to trick you. They ask for money for medicine that does not work.

Rich Romans often employ their own doctor. He is a servant who lives with them.

MEMPHI   GLEGORI

Avoid having an operation! Roman doctors have very basic surgical instruments, such as the ones above.

Pray

You can always go to a temple and pray to **Asklepios**, the god of medicine. Some doctors give you a prayer to go with your medicine, to make it more powerful.

Bone drilling

Bone drills are used to get things like weapons out of bone. They look like corkscrews. You do not get a painkiller when a doctor uses a bone drill on you.

GLOSSARY

amphitheatre a large, circular building like a football stadium. Many forms of entertainment took place in amphitheatres

Asklepios the Greek god of medicine. The Romans decided to use him as their god of medicine too

banquet a meal in which many courses of food are served over many hours

denarii Roman coins made of silver

Latin the language of Rome and the Roman Empire

merchants people who travel to buy and sell goods

mosaics wall, floor, or ceiling pictures made up of tiny squares of coloured tile, stone, or glass

Pantheon a temple built in Rome from about AD 125, during the reign of the Emperor Hadrian

reins thin lengths of leather fixed around a horse's head at one end and held by a driver at the other end to control the horse

sacrifices to kill animals in honour of gods

Trajan Emperor from AD 98 to 117. A great general and also known for his building projects in Rome

trident a spear with three spikes

villas the Roman name for rich people's houses in the country

FURTHER INFORMATION

Websites

Visit the Museum of London website to find out more about the Romans.

www.museumoflondon.org

Visit Chedworth Roman Villa online at:

www.nationaltrust.org.uk

Find out more about Roman underfloor heating and make your own Roman mosaic at:

www.english-heritage.org.uk

Books

You Wouldn't Want To Be a Roman Gladiator by Kathryn Bentor. Wayland (2007).

The Ancient Romans by Anita Ganeri. Wayland (2008).

The Romans (Footsteps). Franklin Watts (2008).

Everyday Life in Roman Times (Clues to the Past). Franklin Watts (2008).

INDEX